Heidi
Activity Book

Written by Catrin Morris

Song lyrics on page 16 written by Pippa Mayfield

Illustrated by Tamsin Hinrichsen

 Singing *   Reading  Speaking   Critical thinking

 Spelling   Writing   Listening *

* To complete these activities, listen to tracks 2, 3, and 4 of the audio download available at **www.ladybird.com/ladybirdreaders**

Look and read. Circle the correct words.

1

a Aunt Dete

b Clara

c Heidi

2

a Clara's father

b Grandfather

c Peter

3

a maid

b goat

c doctor

4

a chair

b doll's house

c wheelchair

2 Find the words and write them on the lines.

ltuosgoatfhohdftmountainsfntGrandmotherkspfjilbtabAuntDeteyloxwheelchairjijzdoGrandfatherjpirhng

1

goat

2

....

3

....

4

....

5

....

6

....

3 Look, match, and write the words.

1 | au | tain

2 | Grand | id

3 | ma | father

4 | wheel | nt

5 | Grand | chair

6 | moun | mother

1   aunt

2 _____

3 _____

4 _____

5 _____

6 _____

4 Look at the pictures and write the words from the box on the lines. 📖 ✏️

| beautiful | happy | little | sad | worried |

1  Heidi's grandfather looked _worried_.

2  Grandfather made her a _____ bed in the roof of the house.

3  There are so many _____ trees and flowers in the mountains.

4  Grandfather was very _____, because he loved Heidi.

5  Grandfather and Peter were very _____ to see Heidi.

5 **Listen and put a ✓ by the correct sentences.** *

1 a Peter looked after the goats on the mountain.

☐

  b They walked to Grandfather's house on
    the mountain.

✓

2 a "You must go to school."

☐

  b "You must stay here."

☐

3 a "She can stay here."

☐

  b "She can't stay here."

☐

4 a Heidi was happy living in the mountains.

☐

  b Heidi wasn't happy living in Frankfurt.

☐

5 a She liked looking after the goats with Peter.

☐

  b She liked a little white goat the most.

☐

6 a "I'll miss you, too."

☐

  b "I missed you, too."

☐

 * To complete this activity, listen to track 2 of the audio download available at www.ladybird.com/ladybirdreaders

6 Write *can*, *can't*, *could*, or *couldn't*.

1 "She .... *can't* .... stay here, I'm much too old."

2 Sometimes, Heidi went to see Peter's grandmother, who .... see.

3 Suddenly, Clara .... walk by herself.

4 "You .... walk!" said Clara's father. "This is the happiest day of my life."

7 Match the two parts of the sentences.

1 "Today, we will go

and walking at the same time!"

2 "There are so many beautiful trees

and see your grandfather."

3 "Last night, the maid saw

and never go back to Frankfurt."

4 "Heidi, you were sleeping

and flowers in the mountains."

5 "I want to stay in the mountains,

a ghost on the stairs."

8 Work with a friend. You are Heidi and your friend is Peter. Ask and answer questions using the words below. 🗨

1

What is your name?

My name is Heidi.

2 who | live with?

3 which goat | like?

4 mountains | cities | best?

9 **Look and read. Put a** **by the correct pictures.**

1 People don't live in this house.

2 This is Heidi's favorite goat.

3 She wants Heidi to go to school in Frankfurt.

4 This helps Clara move around.

10 Read the sentences. Write *so* or *although*.

1 Heidi and her Aunt Dete wanted to visit Heidi's grandfather, _____so_____ they walked up the mountain.

2 Heidi stayed with her grandfather, _____ he was worried about looking after her.

3 Heidi's grandfather made her a little bed, _____ she could sleep in the roof.

4 Peter's grandmother couldn't see, _____ Heidi told her about the beautiful trees.

5 Heidi had to go to Frankfurt, _____ she wanted to stay with her grandfather and Peter.

6 _____ she was happy in Clara's house, Heidi dreamed about the mountains every night.

11 Use *First*, *Next*, *After that*, and *Finally* to write the story. 📖 ✏️

Clara came to visit Heidi, and started to walk again.

Heidi went to stay with her grandfather in the mountains.

Heidi went home because she missed her grandfather, Peter, and the goats.

She stayed with Clara's family in Frankfurt while she went to school.

First, Heidi went to stay with her grandfather in the mountains.

12 Listen and write. Who said this? *

Aunt Dete

Clara

Clara's father

Grandfather

Peter

Heidi

1   Grandfather

2

3

4

5

6

13 Work with a friend. Talk about the picture. Use *There is* or *There are*, and then *on*, *in*, *behind*, *above*, *near*, *in front of*, and *next to*.

1 **There are** three people **in** the room.

2 . . . two pictures . . .

3 . . . some flowers . . .

4 . . . sitting in a wheelchair . . .

14 Look and read. Choose the correct words and write them on the lines. 📖 ✏️ ❓

aunt

doctor

friend

grandfather

grandmother

maid

People in your family:

aunt,

People not in your family:

Heidi went to live with her grandfather.
She liked the trees, she liked the flowers.
She liked her friend Peter, and his goats.
She was happy there in the mountains.
Her aunt said, "Heidi, you must go to school.
You can stay with my friends in Frankfurt."
Heidi liked Clara, her friend in a wheelchair,
but still she dreamed about the mountains.

The maid saw a ghost.
Clara's father wanted to wait for the ghost.
The ghost was Heidi, walking while she slept!
She was dreaming about the mountains!
Heidi went back to her grandfather.
He and Peter were happy to see her.
"I never want to go back to Frankfurt," she said.
"I want to stay here in the mountains."

Clara's father had to go away,
so Clara went to stay with Heidi.
Peter wasn't happy – she was always with Clara!
He pushed Clara's chair down the mountain.
Clara said, "I must try to walk,"
and Heidi and her grandfather helped.
Clara's father saw her walk
and everyone was happy in the mountains!